Section A
Language acquisition

This is a broad topic that covers the ways in which children acquire language from 0 to 11 years. It involves looking at early spoken acquisition in the first few months of a child's life, right up to the point when most children are reading and writing quite fluently by the end of primary school.

A huge amount of language development takes place between birth and 11 years, and you are expected to use your understanding of language methods, concepts, and a grasp of context to analyse and discuss the extracts you will be given in the exam. These extracts will consist of genuine examples of children's language, either transcribed from conversations and sets of utterances spoken over time, or copied from what they have written.

For example, in the exam you might be faced with a conversation between a child and her mother in which you are asked to analyse the language used between the two participants, so you need to think not just about what the child is saying but also about what her mother is saying to her. You could also be given copies of children's writing to look at and questions asking you to focus on what the child has written and how it reflects the child's development of early literacy. Another area might be children's reading and how they learn this skill.

As with the questions in your AS year for ENGB1, a number of assessment objectives (AOs) are applied to your work, and a number of skills are required on your part to do well.

You are expected to:
- use language methods and analytical skills to discuss texts linguistically
- use ideas from language study — concepts, theories, knowledge of case studies and research — to inform your understanding
- use understanding of contextual factors to interpret the texts with insight
- use language clearly and accurately to express your ideas

Fotolia

In this workbook, the questions that you are set will mirror those in the ENGB3 exam, but alongside the exam-style questions you will also have a number of shorter questions designed to help you to focus on the specific elements that you should consider when putting together your exam-style response. These shorter questions will often focus on skills for specific AOs, but at other times they may ask you to look at specific details of a text that might only be important to *that* text in *that* question.

The first two texts/sets of data that are presented to you are less like the exam-style texts than the subsequent ones because they are designed to give you a quick introduction to some of the key concepts and analytical skills that follow.

Introductory texts

Text A Child–parent conversation extracts

The following four extracts are from separate conversations between a girl (**G**) and her dad (**D**). The girl was 2 years 11 months of age in all four examples. What aspects of child language acquisition do you think are most relevant to focus on in these extracts?

Example 1

Context: Dad drawing curtains at bedtime with daughter.

G: Only mans do dat?

D: What did you say?

G: Only daddies do dat?

Example 2

Context: Dad and daughter talking at breakfast. Dad is putting sheets in washing machine.

G: Why you washing dem?

D: Someone did a wee in the bed.

G: I not did that.

Example 3

Context: Dad and daughter talking at lunchtime.

D: I've got an orange here or an apple. Do you want an orange?

G: I want another one apple.

D: OK.

G: What you doing?

D: This? I'm peeling a potato.

G: Peeling tato?

Example 4

Context: Dad and daughter talking about day at nursery and childminder.

D: How was nursery today?

G: Molly did hit me at nursery. Julie told off her.

Reproduced with thanks to Ruby Clayton

---

1 **What are the most noticeable differences between what the daughter says and what you might expect her to say if she were older in terms of the following linguistic areas?**

    a **Phonology (how sounds are formed)**

....

....

....

....

....

....

b Lexis and semantics (words and their meanings)

....
....
....
....

c Grammar (how words are combined to form phrases and sentences)

....
....
....
....
....
....
....

d Pragmatics and functions of language (how words are used to create literal and implied meanings)

....
....
....
....
....
....

2 What ideas from language study could be applied to the exchanges between child and parent in these examples? For example, which ideas from research, case studies, theories of language acquisition and wider language study might be relevant here?

....
....
....
....
....
....
....
....

3 What contextual factors are worth discussing here and how are they reflected in the language used?

....
....
....

Text B Jack and the beanstalk

The following is a short example of a text written by a 7-year-old girl at home as a piece of independent writing, based on stories she had been doing in class at school. What aspects of child language acquisition do you think are most relevant to focus on in this extract?

Once upon a time there were wasaboy called Jack and his mum caird holly and a cow called cow. JACKS mum said " I went to selle the cow))

Jack set of to the market Suddenly a man poppedout from benihd a tree.

" can I hav your cow?))? said the man

"yes you can but you haf to giv me somfink as well)) said Jack.

"fin I will giv you magic beens)) said the man.

Jack wen+ home " mum I have magic beens?.

"I doht waht magic beens I waht muney)) said Jacks mum.

Jacks mum was angry so she threw the magic beens out the window.

The next day abeen stor groow.

Jack said he will clim it so Jack did.

when he got to the tohe he saw a casol.

"fic I son el af yoo mooh beey in said the giant.

Reproduced with thanks to Ruby Clayton

1 What do you notice about the ways in which the child has used each of the following?

   a Orthography and graphology (how words are spelt, how letters are formed and the layout of words and letters on the page)

   b Lexis and semantics (words and their meanings)

   c Grammar (how words are combined to form phrases and sentences)

2 What ideas from language study could be applied to the child's writing in this example? For example, which ideas from research, case studies, theories of language acquisition and wider language study might be relevant here?

3 **What contextual factors are worth discussing here and how are they reflected in the language used?**

....

....

....

....

....

....

Further texts

Now that you have looked at two short extracts and started to think about the kinds of approaches to language acquisition that are required, you can consider analysing other texts to help develop a range of different skills.

Each of the following four texts (C–F) is an extract from children's spoken or written language. The questions set on each are designed to help you to focus on specific features of children's language and to help you towards a better overall understanding of the topic. Once you have studied these texts and answered the questions on them, you will be given two separate exam-style questions (one on spoken language and the other on written) that will ask you to consider the texts you have just read and to respond in a more developed way to both of them.

Text C Playground conversation

The following is an extract from a conversation between a mother (**M**) and her son (**S**), aged 3 years 6 months, about their trip to the park that morning.

M: We enjoyed our trip to the park this morning, didn't we?

S: Yes.

M: What was your favourite thing in the playground?

S: The playground?

M: Yes, your favourite ride in the playground at the park.

S: I liked the swing.

M: You were going very high, weren't you? I was getting sore arms pushing you.

S: I goed higher and higher.

M: Yes, you went really high.

S: But I didn't want to go in baby swing.

M: No you're a bit too big for the baby swings.

S: Why my too big?

M: Because you're getting older. You're nearly 4 now.

S: Will I be older than the girls soon?

M: No, because they're getting older, too.

S: Are they gownups now?

M: No they're only 7.

S: But they bigger an me.

1 Which features of child-directed speech are these? How would you describe and explain what the parent is doing in each of these instances?

A

B

C

2 Which features of children's language are these? How would you describe and explain each of the highlighted areas in text C?

D

E

F

G

3 What can you say about the ways in which the mother interacts with her son and uses child-directed speech?

4 Which theories of child language or concepts connected to language study are relevant to the language development shown here?

Text D School project

Text D is an extract from a project written by an 8-year-old while on a school field trip. The children were given various tasks to do during the day and were told to write up some of their experiences in the form of a guide to the place they had visited.

Insect hunt

You will need
a big net and sheet.
sweep through
the green grass
with the net.
and empty it out
on the white
sheet. See what
you found. I found
a brown ear wig with 6 legs and a
little, tiny ant.

Fire Salamander

head

black skin

spots to defend

A fire salamander
defends itself with
its orangey colours on
its black back. A salamander
eats wriggly worms
and slimy slugs. A
salamander is an amphibian.

1 Which features of children's language would you focus on in this extract? Which features can you identify that might be worth commenting on?

....
....
....
....
....
....

2 What can you say about the particular form and style in which the child has written this text? How has he tried to use language and images to inform and instruct his readers?

....
....
....
....

3 How might the context of this piece of writing be relevant to what the child has written?

....
....
....
....
....

4 How sophisticated is the child's use of grammar in this extract? Think about how he has used phrases and clauses.

....
....
....
....
....
....

5 Which theories of child language or concepts connected with language study are relevant to the language development shown here?

....
....
....
....
....
....
....

Text E Bedtime story

Text E is a transcript of a conversation between a girl (**G**) and her dad (**D**) reading a book together at bedtime. The girl is 6 years old.

Transcription key

(.)	micropause
(1)	pause of number of seconds in bracket
(*takes breath*)	description of non-verbal actions
[some talking] [some more talking] }	simultaneous talk where brackets show words spoken at same time
bold	emphatic stress
=	latched talk (talk that follows directly on from other speaker's turn with no gap)

G Daisy frown (.) frowned mys (.) [tery]

D [mys**ter**iously]

G Mysteriously (.)

D **Good**.

G And crept unseen into the kitchen Hello Daisy [said Mum]

D [Remember] your full stops, darling.

G And crept unseen into the kitchen (*takes breath*). Hello Daisy said Mum.

D That's it. (.) Good.

G What do you want for tea to (.) to (1) what's that=

D =to**night**

G Tonight (*takes breath*) the ostriches will be swimming in tomato (.) saw (.) sauce this evening, said Daisy which (.) which as any spy k (.) knows means a big por (.) port=

D =portion

G Portion (1) what's that?

D It's like an amount (.) a quantity (.) like a plateful of something.

G A big portion of chicken nuggets and lots of ketchup, please (1). We don't eat chicken do we?

D No.

G We don't eat **any** meat.

D No, but we like ketchup don't we?

G Yeah, but not on its own.

D So why do you think Daisy is talking like that in the story?

G Cos she thinks she's a spy.

D I think that's right. (1) She thinks she's a spy but I don't know if her mum really knows what she's on about.

G She thinks she's crazy.

Daisy frowned mysteriously and crept unseen into the kitchen.
"Hello, Daisy," said Mum. "What do you want for tea tonight?"
"The ostriches will be swimming in tomato sauce this evening," said Daisy.
(Which, as any spy knows, means "a big portion of chicken nuggets and lots of ketchup, please!")

From ***006 and a Bit*** *by Kes Gray and illustrated by Nick Sharrett, published by Red Fox. Reproduced by permission of The Random House Group Limited.*

1 What reading strategies does the girl in this extract appear to be using? What characteristics do you notice in some of her errors?

....

....

....

....

....

....

....

....

2 What can you say about the ways in which the father is interacting with his daughter as she reads?

....

....

....

....

....

....

....

3 In what ways do you think the book has been designed for reading by children? Pick out specific examples.

....

....

....

....

....

....

4 Which theories of child language or concepts connected with language study are relevant to the language development shown here?

....

....

....

....

....

....

....

....

....

Text F Exercise book

Text F consists of two pages taken from the exercise book of a 6½-year-old girl at primary school. The first page is an exercise in writing sentences, while the second page is written as a report of her weekend.

Sentences

Target → To make sure each sentence begins with a capital letter and a full stop at the end also capital letters for names.

Mattie had a cat that was called Timmy. ✓ I really like to Play With Imogen. ✓ At the Weekend I Played with Megan and Joe. ✓ Today is the Day i am going to Bradon's house for tea. ✓ Charlotte and Daniel are very Kind. ✓

---

1 Which features of the following can you identify for discussion in text F above and opposite? What can you say about each one?

a Orthography and graphology

My Weekend

Good use of full stops today, a really good try.

On Saturday I
Went to Bridgnorth.
With My Nanny and
Grandad Mummy Daddy and
Fin. After that I went
to the Jewel of the
Sevan and I went to
the bar. But no Children
where Allowed. ✓

Reproduced with thanks to Mattie and Mandy Shannon.

b Punctuation and sentence construction

....
....
....
....
....

c The teacher's comments and marking

....
....
....
....

2 **Which theories of child language or concepts connected with language study are relevant to the literacy development shown here?**

....

....

....

....

....

....

Tackling exam-style questions on language acquisition

Now you have looked at several shorter texts in detail, it is time to think about how you might answer a more developed exam-style question. In the ENGB3 exam, you are given extracts of data that you need to analyse and use as the basis for discussion.

The mark scheme for the ENGB3 questions is obviously important because it helps you to target key areas and to concentrate your attention on those areas that will get you the most marks.

ENGB3 is assessed using three assessment objectives (AOs):

- AO1: Identify and accurately describe features and patterns of language in the texts set for examination (24 marks)
- AO2: Apply and show understanding of relevant language concepts to the texts set (16 marks)
- AO3: Interpret and explain contextual factors in the texts set (8 marks)

As you can see from the different marks allocated, it is important to get the right balance in your response. The data that are set — the transcripts, the language extracts or the reproductions of written texts — must be at the heart of what you do. It is a bad idea to start with theories you have memorised first and try to apply those to whatever data appear. Instead, work from the data and their contexts out, seeing if you can engage with what is there in front of you before you try to relate it to theory and case studies. Examiners want to see candidates who are genuinely engaging with what is in front of them, rather than trying to use a pre-prepared answer.

You **should** show your understanding of relevant theory and research, but only once you have found suitable applications for it. And while knowing some theory and research will probably involve memorising a few names, examples and concepts, remember that just because you have learnt it, it does not necessarily mean you should use all of it. Be selective!

Mark scheme for ENGB3

When thinking of your responses to the short questions and the longer exam-style questions, it is a good idea to keep the mark scheme in mind. The table opposite shows the general mark scheme produced by AQA for ENGB3.

As you can see, the weighting of the marks is completely different from that in the ENGB1 AS exam, so it is important to think about how this might have an impact on what you write. With AO1 taking up half of the available 48 marks, it is clearly the most important AO, so your close engagement with the language of the text extracts (be they child-language or language-change texts) should be a key priority.

AO1 prioritises 'systematic' approaches in the top bands, and this means that careful planning of your answer is important. You should consider which language methods are most appropriate for the exploration of the text extracts you have been given, and make sure you go into real detail. You are expected to use a more demanding range and depth of analytical methods in your A2 year, so make sure you have consolidated and moved on from what you learnt in your AS course.

Unit 3	General numerical mark scheme: Questions 1, 2, 3 and 4				
Mark	**AO1** Select and apply a range of linguistic methods to communicate relevant knowledge using appropriate terminology and coherent, accurate written expression.	Mark	**AO2** Demonstrate critical understanding of a range of concepts and issues relating to the construction and analysis of meanings in spoken and written language, using knowledge of linguistic approaches.	Mark	**AO3** Analyse and evaluate the influence of contextual factors on the production and reception of spoken and written language, showing knowledge of the key constituents of language.
22–24	Systematic and evaluative exploration of data using linguistic methods. Accurate and perceptive linguistic knowledge. Appropriate, controlled and accurate expression.	15–16	Perceptive understanding of a range of issues. Conceptualised discussion of ideas surrounding topic. Exploration of a range of judicious examples.	8	Perceptive and insightful exploration of contextual factors. Analytical and systematic interpretation of contextual factors in the light of language features. Integrated and helpful use of the data to support interpretation.
16–21	Use of linguistic methods in a systematic way. Appropriate and accurate linguistic knowledge. Controlled and accurate expression.	11–14	Clear understanding of a range of language concepts/issues. Developed discussion of ideas relating to concepts/issues. Exploration of a range of well-selected examples.	6–7	Clear understanding of a range of contextual factors. Sound analysis and engagement with contextual factors in the light of language features. Fully supported interpretations.
10–15	Application and exploration of some linguistic methods. Some appropriate linguistic knowledge. Generally accurate written communication.	7–10	Some awareness of language concepts and issues. A number of concepts/issues discussed — but not fully explored. Beginning to select and use salient examples.	4–5	Some consideration and understanding of contextual factors. Some awareness of the link between language features and content. Ideas generally supported.
4–9	Basic linguistic methods applied, but not convincing. Limited linguistic knowledge/ understanding. Inconsistent clarity and accuracy in communication.	3–6	Limited number of language concepts highlighted. Superficial understanding shown. Often descriptive and/or anecdotal in reference.	2–3	Awareness of one or two factors influencing data — likely to be broad in focus. Some limited attempt to analyse audience/purpose/ genre/context. Some supported points.
1–3	Linguistic methods applied inaccurately or not at all. Rudimentary linguistic knowledge. Lapses in written communication.	1–2	Elementary understanding of language concepts and use. More knowledge than relevance shown. Occasional reference to language concept, but likely to be misunderstood.	1	Little or no attempt to explore issues of audience/purpose/ genre/context. Superficial/generalised response to the data. Likely to paraphrase/summarise.
0	Nothing written, unintelligible.	0	Nothing written, unintelligible.	0	Nothing written, unintelligible.

AO2 is worth 16 marks and covers 'concepts and issues'. You will need to display knowledge of different case studies, research and theories and a wider understanding of stages of child-language development or periods of language-change history.

AO3 is worth 8 marks but can be an important starting-point for you to consider. AO3 relates to the contextual factors that affect a text and its meanings within that context. For child-language acquisition this might mean thinking about the physical environment the child is in, the task he or she is engaged in, the genre he or she is writing in, for example. For language-change, this might relate to the genre of the text, the audience and purpose of the extracts and perhaps the social context. While the weighting of this AO suggests it is less important than the other two, it can make a good starting-point from which to develop your answer.

Theory and research activities

Spoken acquisition theory

As explained above, to get marks for AO2 you need to be able to show that you understand key concepts about this topic, and to do that it is important to have looked at what some of the main thinkers and researchers in the field of language acquisition have said.

The grid below is split into boxes representing each major theory of child-language acquisition. There are spaces left for you to fill in examples from the data you have seen so far in texts A, C and E. You should make a note of where there is potential evidence for one of the theories. This will help you to plan some of the relevant AO2 knowledge that might be applied to these extracts.

For example, if you think that the use of the over-generalisation 'mans' in text A is potentially good

evidence for a nativist (innateness) theory of language acquisition because it shows how a child has deduced a set of rules and then over-applied them to an irregular plural, then note the example in the nativist box with a brief explanation of why it is relevant.

Along with the four key theories (nativist, interactionist, cognitive and behaviourist), you will see boxes for stages (such as the **telegraphic** stage, or the stages of **negative** or **question** formation outlined by Roger Brown, Ursula Bellugi and Jean Peccei, among others). If you see good evidence in texts A, C and E for any of these, make a note. When you come to answer the exam-style question, you can then produce contextualised evidence from some of the texts to help to illustrate your arguments.

Nativist theory	Behaviourist theory
Interactionist theory	Cognitive theory
Two-word stage	Telegraphic stage
Post-telegraphic stage	Question-formation stages
Negative-formation stages	Halliday's functions of language

Reading and writing acquisition theory

A similar grid is available to help you to plan your use of research and topic knowledge in the questions on how children learn to read and write. You will see that the grid contains names of particular researchers and thinkers in the field as well as approaches to reading such as **phonics** and **look and say**. So try to use your textbooks and class notes to make sure you are clear on each of these people and what they proposed (for example, Barry Kroll's stages or Lev Vygotsky's ideas about children's conceptual development and the role of carers and parents in this).

Fill in the grid below with short examples from texts B, D, E and F to help you to plan some of the relevant AO2 knowledge that might be applied to these extracts.

Phonics	Look and say
Kroll's stages	Perera's chronological/non-chronological text types
Britton's modes of writing	Rothery's genres of writing
Spelling stages	Labov's narrative structure
Chall's reading stages	Social interaction theories

Exam-style questions

You are allowed 15 minutes for planning and 1 hour for writing your answer for each of these questions.

Children's spoken language

01 Referring in detail to the transcripts in texts A, C and E and to relevant ideas from language study, analyse the parent and child interactions in these contexts.

`48 marks`

Children's writing

02 Referring in detail to texts B, D and F and to relevant ideas from language study, explore early literacy development.

`48 marks`

Planning sheet for question 1

In the space below — and using the suggested headings if they fit with your way of working — try to plan out your answer to exam-style question 1.

AO3: What is the specific context to each interaction? How might the context influence each interaction? What age is the child in each context?

....

AO1: Which specific features of interaction between parent and child can you note from each transcript and how are they working? Can you group your observations using language methods (phonology, lexis and semantics, grammar and pragmatics)?

Text A

....

Text C

....

....

....

Text E

....

....

....

AO2: Which ideas from language study, case studies and research that you have identified in your planning can be related to these interactions?

....

....

....

....

....

....

....

....

Planning sheet for question 2

In the space below — and using the suggested headings if they fit with your way of working — try to plan out your answer to exam-style question 2.

AO3: What is the specific context to each piece of writing? In response to what have they been produced and in what circumstances are the texts being written? What do we know about the age of each child?

....

....

....

....

....

....

....

....

AO1: Which specific features of literacy development can you identify? What achievements as well as errors have the children made? Can you group your observations using language methods (orthography, graphology, lexis and semantics, grammar and pragmatics)?

Text B

....
....
....
....
....

Text D

....
....
....
....
....

Text F

....
....
....
....
....

AO2: Which ideas from language study, case studies and research that you have identified in your planning can be related to these pieces of writing?

....
....
....
....
....
....
....

Section B Language change

As with language acquisition, this is a big topic and you need to be prepared for a range of different texts in the exam itself. This workbook cannot cover everything in terms of content for this topic, but you can use it to help you to target your revision and hone your skills for many of the types of text that may turn up in the exam.

Language change for ENGB3 covers the period 1700 to the present day, and a great deal of change has happened in that time and is still happening. While the change itself is ongoing — and arguably picking up speed — the skills you need as a student to analyse language change remain relatively consistent and it is these we will concentrate on in this part of the workbook.

For language change this means that you will need to understand how a number of key changes in language use relate to the language methods you have been studying since the beginning of the English Language A-level, and how these methods can be used to unlock texts from different times to see how they work.

It is also important to have an overarching sense of some of the key time periods, processes and patterns across the years specified and how the texts you study in the exam might fit into these. For example, if you are presented with a text from the mid-nineteenth century, you might find it useful to consider how that text might reflect what was happening to English at that time or, more generally, what was happening in society and how the values of the time might be reflected or represented in the text.

Another element of this topic is that of attitudes towards change. Attitudes vary: there are those who embrace change and see it as progress, while others strive to prevent change and see language change as a form of erosion or destruction. Some of the texts chosen in this second section of the workbook will offer you the potential to explore how the texts might reflect such attitudes, or how different camps might view the changes described or exemplified within them.

As with the first section of this workbook, the first few texts (G–L) will be designed to help you to focus your attention on specific language features and concepts, before offering you a wider focus on longer, more developed texts, which can be used for exam-style answers.

Introductory texts

Text G Eighteenth century literature

The following text is an extract from a novel, *The Expedition of Humphry Clinker*, by Tobias Smollett, published in 1771. Read the extract and then answer the questions that follow.

Now, mark the contrast at London. I am pent up in frowsy lodgings where there is not room enough to swing a cat, and I breathe the steams of endless putrefaction; and these would undoubtedly produce a pestilence if they were not qualified by the gross acid of sea coal, which is itself a pernicious nuisance to lungs of any delicacy of texture. But even this boasted corrector cannot prevent those languid sallow looks that distinguish the inhabitants of London from those ruddy swains that lead a country life. I go to bed after midnight, jaded and restless from the dissipation of the day. I start every hour from my sleep at the horrid noise of the watchmen bawling the hour through every street, and thundering at every door — a set of useless fellows, who serve no other purpose but that of disturbing the repose of the inhabitants — and by five o'clock I start out of bed, in consequence of the still more dreadful alarm made by the country carts and noisy rustics bellowing green peas under my window. If I would drink water, I must quaff the mawkish contents of an open aqueduct, exposed to all manner of defilement, or swallow that which comes from the river Thames, impregnated with all the filth of London and Westminster. Human excrement is the least offensive part of the concrete, which is composed of all the drugs, minerals, and poisons used in mechanics and manufactures, enriched with the putrefying carcasses of beasts and men, and mixed with the scourings of all the washtubs, kennels, and common sewers, within the bills of mortality.

This is the agreeable potation extolled by the Londoners as the finest water in the universe. As to the intoxicating potion sold for wine, it is a vile, unpalatable, and pernicious sophistication, balderdashed with cider, corn spit, and the juice of sloes. In an action at law, laid against a carman for having staved a cask of port, it appeared, from the evidence of the cooper, that there were not above five gallons of real wine in the whole pipe, which held above a hundred — and even that had been brewed and adulterated by the merchant at Oporto. The bread I eat in London is a deleterious paste, mixed up with chalk, alum, and bone ashes, insipid to the taste and destructive to the constitution. The good people are not ignorant of this adulteration, but they prefer it to wholesome bread, because it is whiter than the meal of corn. Thus they sacrifice their taste and their health, and the lives of their tender infants, to a most absurd gratification of a misjudging eye, and the miller or baker is obliged to poison them and their families in order to live by his profession.

1 **What kinds of attitudes does the narrator express towards his experiences in London? Try to find examples where you can identify a particular view being expressed.**

....
....
....
....
....
....

2 **How different are the lexis (vocabulary) and semantics (word meanings) compared with what you might read in a novel in the present day?**

....
....
....
....
....
....
....

3 **In terms of the text's grammar, do you notice any differences between what is written here and modern word order or sentence structure?**

....
....
....
....
....
....

4 To what extent might the period when this text was written have influenced some of the language features you have noticed?

....

....

....

....

....

Text H Early twentieth century advertising

This text is an advertisement for a box of Kellogg's All-Bran cereal, produced in 1928.

Thousands of Doctors Prescribe
Kellogg's All-Bran for Constipation

IT is terrible—the toll that constipation takes in health and happiness. It thieves beauty. It wrecks vitality. It is the cause of much suffering and disease. And all the while it could be so easily relieved! Kellogg's ALL-BRAN is guaranteed to relieve constipation—safely, permanently.

Doctors recommend ALL-BRAN because it is 100% bran. They know that 100% bran means 100% results.

ALL-BRAN carries through the system moisture which its "bulk" absorbs. And it gently distends the intestines—cleansing, removing wastes.

Eat at least two tablespoonfuls of Kellogg's ALL-BRAN every day—in chronic cases with every meal. Serve ALL-BRAN with cold milk or cream—and add fruits if desired.

Sold by all Grocers

KELLOGG COMPANY of GREAT BRITAIN, Ltd.
329, High Holborn
London, W. C. 1

Made by Kellogg in London, Canada

Ad 4

Jeff Morgan 01/Alamy

25

This text is taken from the box of Dorset Cereals' *Simply Delicious Muesli*, produced in 2012.

everyday breakfast pleasure

30% fruit, nuts & seeds

dorset cereals®
simply delicious muesli
18 glorious bowlfuls 850g℮

dorset cereals®
honest, tasty and real

win... lovely things

Play our Spin the Bottle game and you could win wonderful prizes, every week. We're talking breakfast-in-bed sets, lovely farm holidays... that sort of thing. So why not change your arm today? Just go to our homepage and give it a spin.

www.dorsetcereals.co.uk

a simple blend of roasted hazelnuts, brazil nuts & moreish flakes, with juicy raisins & dates

simple, but then the best things in life usually are

simply delicious muesli
A blend of multigrain flakes with dried fruit, nuts and sunflower seeds

good to know
▶ High in fibre
▶ Contains wholegrains
▶ No added preservatives
▶ No added sugar
▶ Contains naturally occurring sugars
▶ A low sodium food
▶ Vegetarian Society approved

ingredients
Dried fruit sultanas (28%) [raisins, sultanas, dates, pineapple], whole roasted hazelnut [nut], flakes, wheat flakes, barley flakes, toasted and malted wheat flakes (wheat, barley malt extract), sunflower seeds (4%).

⚠ allergy advice
Please see ingredients for allergens. May contain other nuts and milk

We use only the best, natural ingredients and this means sometimes a stray piece of shell or fruit stone may sneak past our checks and into your bowl.

best enjoyed
Serve with milk, yoghurt or fruit juice for a delicious and nutritious breakfast.

storage instructions
Store in a cool, dry place. Some of the best bits may have settled at the bottom of the pack, so please shake gently before opening. For best before end date, see base of pack.

Woodland trust
We're supporting the Woodland Trust's Jubilee Woodproject, which is helping people across the UK plant 6 million trees. To find out more, just visit: www.dorsetcereals.co.uk/trees

nutritional information

typical values		100g	46g as sold serving*
Energy	kJ	1,600	981
	kcal	366	219
Protein		9.9g	8.7g
Carbohydrate		68.1g	31.7g
- of which sugars		16.8g	13.2g
Fat		7.4g	4.6g
- of which saturates		1.1g	1.8g
- monounsaturates		3.9g	2.3g
- polyunsaturates		2.0g	1.0g
Fibre		8.9g	4.0g
Sodium		0.08g	0.10g
- equivalent as salt		0.20g	0.25g

*a serving includes 126ml of semi-skimmed milk

eat it then tweet it
Let the world know which cereal you're munching and you could win a fantastic prize. Just follow us @dorsetcereals and tweet a message with the #simplydelicious hashtag.

850g℮

1 What audiences and purposes would you identify for texts H and I?

....

....

....

....

....

....

....

2 What features of graphology do you think are worth commenting on in the two texts?

....

....

....

....

....

3 In terms of the grammatical, lexical and semantic choices in each text, do you notice any major differences?

....

....

....

....

....

....

....

....

....

....

....

4 To what extent do you think the time period these texts were produced in might have influenced the language being used?

....

....

....

....

....

....

....

....

Text J Nineteenth century household management

This is the preface to Isabella Beeton's *Book of Household Management*, first published in 1861.

I must frankly own, that if I had known, beforehand, that this book would have cost me the labour which it has, I should never have been courageous enough to commence it. What moved me, in the first instance, to attempt a work like this, was the discomfort and suffering which I had seen brought upon men and women by household mismanagement. I have always thought that there is no more fruitful source of family discontent than a housewife's badly cooked dinners and untidy ways. Men are now so well served out of doors—at their clubs, well-ordered taverns, and dining-houses, that in order to compete with the attractions of these places, a mistress must be thoroughly acquainted with the theory and practice of cookery, as well as be perfectly conversant with all the other arts of making and keeping a comfortable home.

In this book I have attempted to give, under the chapters devoted to cookery, an intelligible arrangement to every recipe, a list of the ingredients, a plain statement of the mode of preparing each dish, and a careful estimate of its cost, the number of people for whom it is sufficient, and the time when it is seasonable. For the matter of the recipes, I am indebted, in some measure, to many correspondents of the 'Englishwoman's Domestic Magazine,' who have obligingly placed at my disposal their formulas for many original preparations. A large private circle has also rendered me considerable service. A diligent study of the works of the best modern writers on cookery was also necessary to the faithful fulfilment of my task. Friends in England, Scotland, Ireland, France, and Germany, have also very materially aided me. I have paid great attention to those recipes which come under the head of 'COLD MEAT COOKERY.' But in the department belonging to the Cook I have striven, too, to make my work something more than a Cookery Book, and have, therefore, on the best authority that I could obtain, given an account of the natural history of the animals and vegetables which we use as food. I have followed the animal from his birth to his appearance on the table; have described the manner of feeding him, and of slaying him, the position of his various joints, and, after giving the recipes, have described the modes of carving Meat, Poultry, and Game. Skilful artists have designed the numerous drawings which appear in this work, and which illustrate, better than any description, many important and interesting items. The coloured plates are a novelty not without value.

Besides the great portion of the book which has especial reference to the cook's department, there are chapters devoted to those of the other servants of the household, who have all, I trust, their duties clearly assigned to them.

Towards the end of the work will be found valuable chapters on the 'Management of Children'——'The Doctor,' the latter principally referring to accidents and emergencies, some of which are certain to occur in the experience of every one of us; and the last chapter contains 'Legal Memoranda,' which will be serviceable in cases of doubt as to the proper course to be adopted in the relations between Landlord and Tenant, Tax-gatherer and Tax-payer, and Tradesman and Customer.

These chapters have been contributed by gentlemen fully entitled to confidence; those on medical subjects by an experienced surgeon, and the legal matter by a solicitor.

I wish here to acknowledge the kind letters and congratulations I have received during the progress of this work, and have only further to add, that I trust the result of the four years' incessant labour which I have expended will not be altogether unacceptable to some of my countrymen and countrywomen.

Text K How To Be A Woman

This text is the back cover from Caitlin Moran's *How To Be A Woman*, first published in 2011.

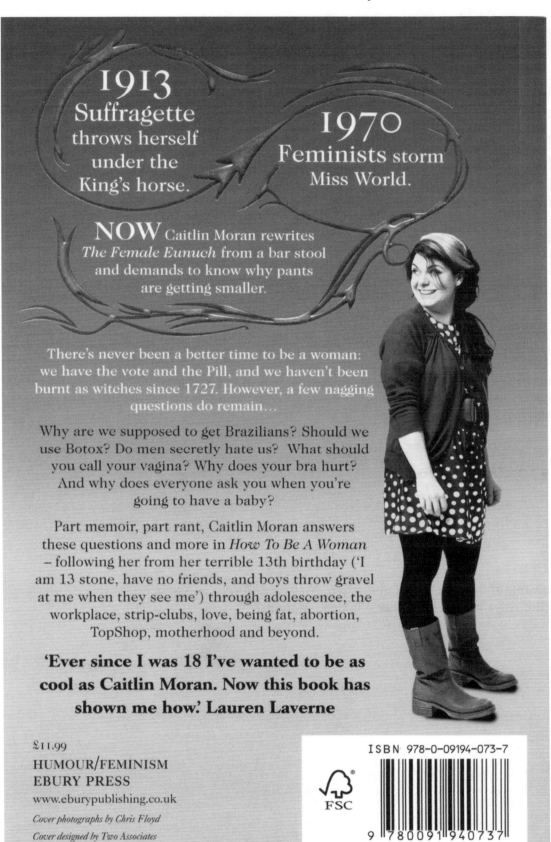

1913
Suffragette throws herself under the King's horse.

1970
Feminists storm Miss World.

NOW Caitlin Moran rewrites *The Female Eunuch* from a bar stool and demands to know why pants are getting smaller.

There's never been a better time to be a woman: we have the vote and the Pill, and we haven't been burnt as witches since 1727. However, a few nagging questions do remain…

Why are we supposed to get Brazilians? Should we use Botox? Do men secretly hate us? What should you call your vagina? Why does your bra hurt? And why does everyone ask you when you're going to have a baby?

Part memoir, part rant, Caitlin Moran answers these questions and more in *How To Be A Woman* – following her from her terrible 13th birthday ('I am 13 stone, have no friends, and boys throw gravel at me when they see me') through adolescence, the workplace, strip-clubs, love, being fat, abortion, TopShop, motherhood and beyond.

'Ever since I was 18 I've wanted to be as cool as Caitlin Moran. Now this book has shown me how.' Lauren Laverne

£11.99
HUMOUR/FEMINISM
EBURY PRESS
www.eburypublishing.co.uk
Cover photographs by Chris Floyd
Cover designed by Two Associates

FSC

ISBN 978-0-09194-073-7

9 780091 940737

From How To Be A Woman by Caitlin Moran, published by Ebury Press. Reproduced by permission of The Random House Group Limited

1 Where would be a good point to start with the contexts in which texts **J** and **K** were produced? How important do you think the context to each might be when comparing them?

....
....
....
....
....

2 The tone and style of these texts is clearly different. What specific examples could you refer to in order to illustrate the differences between them?

....
....
....
....
....
....
....

3 The writers of both texts make references to a range of things that they assume their readers will understand. What do these references tell us about the different attitudes shown in each text?

....
....
....
....

4 How might the readers of these two texts be different and how might this be linked to some of the ways in which language is used in them?

....
....
....
....
....

Further texts

Tackling exam-style questions on language change

Now you've had a close look at some examples of language change texts, it is time to think about how you might approach an exam-style question. For the first question of this type, a comparison question, you will need to read both texts L and M.

ENGB3 exam papers often feature comparative questions, where similar subject matter is handled in different ways by texts from different time periods. Here you have been given a modern advert for a videogame and an older one from the mid-twentieth century for a toy-building set.

In the exam-style questions that follow the next two sets of texts (L and M; N and O) you will need to think about the ways in which language is used to communicate in each text and how language has changed over time. You will be given some suggestions about how to plan and answer a question like this in the notes that follow each exam-style question.

Text L Earth depends on you

This text is an e-mail that formed part of an advertising campaign for the videogame Mass Effect 3, sent to EA Games subscribers in 2012.

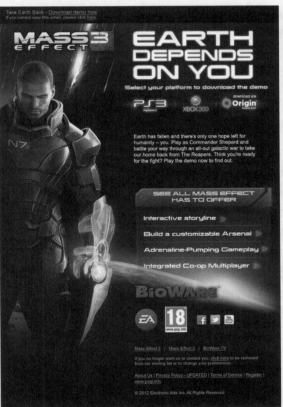

Take Earth Back - <u>Download demo now</u>

If you cannot view this e-mail, please click <u>here</u>

MASS EFFECT 3   EARTH DEPENDS ON YOU

Select your platform to download the demo

<u>PS3</u>   <u>XBox360</u>   <u>download via Origin</u>

Earth has fallen and there's only one hope left for humanity — you. Play as Commander Shepard and battle your way through an all-out galactic war to take our home back from The Reapers. Think you're ready for the fight? Play the demo now to find out.

SEE ALL MASS EFFECT HAS TO OFFER

Interactive storyline ▷

Build a customizable Arsenal ▷

Adrenaline-Pumping Gameplay ▷

Integrated Co-op Multiplayer ▷

<u>Mass Effect 3</u> □   <u>Mass Effect 2</u> □   <u>BioWare TV</u>

If you no longer want us to contact you, click here to be removed from our mailing list or to change your preferences.

<u>About Us</u> □   <u>Privacy Policy - Updated</u> □
<u>Terms of Service</u> □   <u>Register</u> □   <u>www.pegi.info</u>

31

This text is an advertisement for a children's toy, produced by the games company J. W. Spear & Sons in 1955.

Build the _real_ thing —

with **BRICKPLAYER**

BRICK and MORTAR BUILDING KIT and ACCESSORIES

Brickplayer Kit 3	.. .. ..	25/6
Brickplayer Kit 4	.. .. ..	47/6
Kit 3A converting Kit 3 into Kit 4		25/6
Brickplayer Farm Kit	.. ..	56/6
2,000 Bricks Box	.. .. ..	53/6

Extra Bricks, Roofing and Cement in low priced packs.

Windows and Doors obtainable singly.

The Brickplayer Kit contains miniature bricks in all required shapes, mortar, roofing, plastic windows and doors, plans, and instruction booklet. All models are architect designed to '0' gauge scale. Buildings can be permanent or dismantled by merely soaking in water and the bricks used again and again.

If your dealer cannot supply, write for leaflet and address of nearest stockist to:

J. W. SPEAR & SONS LTD.
DEPT. M • ENFIELD • MIDDLESEX

YOUR IDEAL XMAS GIFT

Jeff Morgan 12/Alamy

Exam-style question

Referring to texts L and M in detail, and to relevant ideas from language study, analyse the ways language has changed over time. **48 marks**

The mark scheme for ENGB3 is again important here, because it helps you to target key areas and to concentrate your attention on those areas that will get you the most marks.

ENGB3 is assessed using three assessment objectives (AOs):

- **AO1: Identify and accurately describe features and patterns of language in the texts set for examination** **24 marks**
- **AO2: Apply (and show understanding of) relevant language concepts to the texts set** **16 marks**
- **AO3: Interpret and explain contextual factors in the texts set** **8 marks**

Refer to the marks table on page 17. As you will see from the different marks allocated, it is important to get the right balance in your response. The data that are set — the extracts from different texts — must be at the heart of what you do. While at some point you should show your knowledge and understanding of how language has changed over time by referring to key developments and important figures in the history of language change, examiners do not want to see you offload everything you know about Caxton's printing press, Johnson's Dictionary, Bishop Lowth's Grammar or the history of Britain's colonial expansion.

It is probably a good idea to start with the texts and then move on to the historical periods. Many successful candidates begin their responses with a quick look at the genre, audience, subject and purpose of the texts (**GASP**).

Genre: what type of text is it? Which genre does it fall into and how might this influence its language and structure?

Audience: who are the texts aimed at and how can we tell?

Subject: what are the texts about? This may seem straightforward, but it can often be a helpful exercise to try to summarise in your own words what you think the texts are actually about. You can then identify key words and fields related to the subject matter.

Purpose: why have the texts been written and does this have any bearing on the choices of language and structure?

Although some of the texts may look different from modern writing, they may nevertheless have been written by people with similar thoughts and feelings to those of a modern reader. Try to use some of the skills of textual analysis you have developed in your AS year and since, and *then* think about how you can also introduce the aspects of language change that are so important to this topic.

Addressing AO2: using ideas from language study

What are the most relevant aspects of language change relating to these two texts? Some suggestions for questions you might want to ask are:

- How has technology shaped the ways in which we use language in advertising?
- How have modes of communication changed in the period between these two texts being published?
- What wider changes in language can be related to these two texts? Do they fit into any overarching patterns of language change that might have existed before the date of text M?

Plan and write your answer on separate sheets of paper.

This text is taken from the rules of a school in London, *c.* 1892.

Brondesbury and Kilburn High School.

————————

RULES.

1. Every girl will be late, morning and afternoon, who is not in the Hall before the door is bolted.

2. Every girl must wear the School hat-band and hair ribbon and the Regulation Drill dress (Summer or Winter blouse).

3. Every girl must change her shoes when she comes to School and when she goes into the Playground. No india-rubber shoes may be worn, except for drill.

4. After the second bell, girls are to be <u>in their seats</u>, and silent.

5. No girl may speak in the break-line, nor when she goes back to her Class-room after break.

6. No girl may be in the Class-rooms out of class-hours.

7. No girl is allowed to go into any Cloak-room but her own, nor to play in the Cloak-rooms at any time, nor to speak in the Cloak-rooms without permission.

8. No conversation nor loitering is allowed in the Lavatories, nor running about in the Dining-room.

9. No girl may stay in School after 1.10 p.m., nor after 4.10 p.m. except with special permission.

10. Girls must not write on the blackboards without leave. Girls who wilfully misuse desks or other School property must pay for necessary repairs.

11. No work may be given in late.

12. No absence and no lesson will be excused unless <u>a good reason, stated in writing</u>, be brought to the Head-Mistress, on the following day.

Reproduced by permission of Brent Archives

Text O College code of conduct

This text is adapted from the student handbook of a sixth-form college in the UK in 2011.

STUDENT CODE OF CONDUCT

As a student at The National College you will be given all the support and guidance you need to ensure that you achieve success. The Code of Conduct is a guide showing you what we expect from all students at the College so that we can help you to achieve in a supportive, caring and non-threatening environment.

1 Behave towards all staff and other students in a way that does not offend. Avoid using foul or abusive language, and avoid racist, sexist and anti-social behaviour (such as spitting). This applies to all areas of the College premises and on transport to and from the College.

2 Dress in a way that does not offend others. No hoods should be worn up in college and no form of headgear (including baseball caps, hats or scarves) may be worn in classrooms, studios, workshops or any other teaching areas unless for medical or religious reasons.

3 Seek help if needed.

4 Treat everyone with respect. Any form of bullying will be treated extremely seriously and may lead to permanent exclusion from the College.

5 Be punctual and attend all lessons (unless your absence has been agreed in advance and through the proper channels).

6 Inform your tutor if you are absent or likely to be unavoidably late.

7 Agree with your tutor what you need to do to catch up if you have been absent.

8 Work to the best of your ability in class and ensure that you do not interfere with the learning of others.

9 Complete punctually all work set outside the lesson.

10 Meet deadlines for all work.

11 Make sure all work produced for assignments and exams is your own work. Information used from another source must be referenced appropriately. Plagiarism and/or cheating may lead to disciplinary action by the College and/or Awarding Body/Examinations Board.

12 Treat all College property with respect.

13 Wear or carry your ID badge at all times and be prepared to show it to any member of staff if asked.

14 Follow the College's Health and Safety rules at all times.

15 Switch off your mobile phone in class. Students whose phone use interferes with class discipline may have their equipment confiscated and returned at the end of the day.

16 Do not take food or drink (apart from bottled water) into classrooms, workshops or sports areas.

17 Smoking is a harmful and anti-social habit and is discouraged by the College. If you wish to smoke, please do so only in designated smoking areas. Smoking is not permitted outside the College gates.

18 Dispose of your litter responsibly by using bins and recycling zones located in and around the College.

Exam-style question

Referring to texts N and O in detail, and to relevant ideas from language study, analyse the ways language has changed over time.

48 marks

Planning your answer

As with the question on texts L and M, you can apply an initial GASP framework to these two texts before considering the language change factors that might be relevant. Some suggestions are:

■ There is a more marked time gap between texts N and O than L and M. What relevant changes to English in the intervening period could you refer to?

■ What social changes have taken place that might have had an impact on how the texts address their target audiences?

Attitudes to language change

Another type of question that might appear for language change on ENGB3 is one that concerns how people feel about language change and how this relates to wider discussions and debates about the language.

The text that follows offers you the chance to relate what you know about different attitudes to a discussion about new words, who uses them and how they are used.

Text P Proper hench

This text is an article from the *Mail Online* from 2008 about slang words entering the language.

'Check me out, I'm proper hench': New dictionary helps parents understand teenglish language

To some it might seem blindingly bait, but for parents of teenage bluds their conversations could soon become a lot clearer.

The jargon-buster website contains almost a hundred definitions of words commonly used by teenagers but until now incomprehensible to their parents.

Among them is 'chirps' (to chat up); 'dry' (boring); 'nang', which translates as brilliant; and 'off the hook' — a phrase to describe something as excellent.

Devised by the charity Parentline Plus, the gotateenager website was created to help parents to understand their children better and remove the language barrier.

They spent months talking to parents and teenagers about the latest slang before compiling the online dictionary of 96 words from 'bare' — meaning many — to 'wagwaan', or what's going on?

Other words include 'phat' (cool), 'tight' (close), 'bluds' (friends), 'bait' (obvious), 'butters' (ugly) and 'rents' (parents). There are also translations of 'on their jays' (on their own), 'flossing' (showing off) and 'hench' (to be strong).

Nikola Mann, who helped to create the site, said: 'It makes you realise how out of touch you can get when you read some of the words teenagers are using now.

'The jargon buster is simply light-hearted and fun, but it was actually something parents asked us for when we were designing the site.

'It grew out of conversations we were having with parents on our free 24-hour helpline who were struggling to understand their children and wanted to know what words used by their teenagers actually meant.'

THOSE WORDS EXPLAINED

bait obvious	**dry** boring	**nang** brilliant
beef problem	**dissed** disrespected	**neeky** nerdy/geeky
blaze smoke	**endz** neighbourhood	**off the hook** excellent
blud friend, mate	**feds** police	**on your jays** alone
buff attractive	**flossing** showing off	**papers** money
butters ugly	**gaged** robbed	**phat** cool, great
clock catch out	**hench** strong	**player** love cheat
cotching chilling out	**jacked** stolen	**rents** parents
crunk crazy, drunk	**jook** to stab or steal	
deep bad	**murk** kill or injure	

'One of the main messages we're trying to get across is that the key to a good relationship between parents and teenagers is communication and the jargon buster is all about improving that.'

The website also includes a host of features, from e-learning modules and courses in dealing with drug and alcohol use to an online comic book with storylines and scenarios familiar to many teens.

Topics covered include drugs, sex, bullying, boundaries, health, school and self-confidence.

The site also boasts blogs, message boards, stories, a texting service with tips and information, and a live web TV show. The first of four shows will go online on Monday.

It also hopes to give the likes of Facebook a run for its money by giving the parents of teens the chance to chat online and support one another.

Maureen Pearson, an area manager for Parentline Plus, added: 'Parents of primary-school children enjoy a network of support and friendship that is lost when their children make the transition to secondary school.

'Gotateenager.org.uk plugs that gap by creating an online community for parents of teenagers.'

The charity offers a free 24-hour confidential hotline on 0808 800 2222 to parents, who can also log on to www.parentlineplus.org.uk or www.gotateenager.org.uk for advice.

http://www.dailymail.co.uk/news/article-1054167/Check-Im-proper-hench-New-dictionary-helps-parents-understand-teenglish-language.html

© Daily Mail (Reproduced by permission of Solo Syndication)

Exam-style question

You are allowed 15 minutes for planning and 1 hour for writing your answer to this question.

Referring in detail to text P and to relevant ideas from language study, explore how attitudes to language alter over time, how language changes and how these changes are reported.

48 marks

Text Q Tweeting the riots

Text Q consists of a series of tweets by national newspaper journalist Paul Lewis on the night of 6 August 2011 as he reported events during the first night of rioting in North London, after the police shot Mark Duggan. (Reproduced by permission of Paul Lewis.)

 Paul Lewis ✓   **Edit your profile**

3,714 TWEETS
581 FOLLOWING
46,520 FOLLOWERS

PaulLewis : Sat Aug 06 22:12:50
Where exactly in Tottenham is the riot happening? Street name?

PaulLewis : Sat Aug 06 22:23
City of London police sending reinforcements to Tottenham riot

PaulLewis : Sat Aug 06 22:24
All roads north Seven Sisters station blocked off due to Tottenham riot

PaulLewis : Sat Aug 06 22:25
I'm heading to Tottenham riot. Advice anyone?

PaulLewis : Sat Aug 06 22:30
Police horses at Seven Sisters heading toward Tottenham riot

PaulLewis : Sat Aug 06 22:36
Tottenham riot road blocked http://yfrog.com/kk7idmlj

PaulLewis : Sat Aug 06 22:40
Hi Fi video store looted on tottenham high road

PaulLewis : Sat Aug 06 22:41
I swear this is true. Just saw kid looting a lute. #tottenhamriot

PaulLewis : Sat Aug 06 22:43
Totteham riot. Chants of 'we want answers' http://yfrog.com/hswbgyzj

PaulLewis : Sat Aug 06 22:44
Shops across Tottenham high road smashed and ransacked. Some looting electrical equipment. #riot

PaulLewis : Sat Aug 06 22:46
Store using crates of plastic bottles of water to defend windows. #tottenhamriot http://yfrog.com/gygboooj

PaulLewis : Sat Aug 06 22:56
Rioters sent sprinting after another charge. Whole building in flames. #tottenhamriot http://yfrog.com/khzcgvtj

PaulLewis : Sat Aug 06 32:05
If police indeed are saying #tottenhamriot 'contained', that is absolutely not true. It is mayhem.

PaulLewis : Sat Aug 06 23:13
Loud bangs now in #tottenhamriot. TV cameras well outside cordon. Police van arriving pelted with bricks.

PaulLewis : Sat Aug 06 23:16
Jeers of 'You took your time' as two fire engines enter scene of #tottenhamriot

PaulLewis : Sat Aug 06 00:18
Young people here all swapping blackberry message accounts of Mark Duggan shooting. tottenham

PaulLewis : Sat Aug 06 00:54
Riots appear to have move to estate north-west of high road, which is now under police control. I'm off home. #tottenhamriot

PaulLewis : Sat Aug 06 00:55
Spking to young men in side-streets u get real sense of how rumour fills vacuum during controversial police shootings. #tottenhamriot

PaulLewis : Sun Aug 07 01:09
BBC/ABC/Al-Jazeera all asked me during live interviews tonight about ethnic make-up of #tottenhamriot

PaulLewis : Sun Aug 07 02:24
ALDI supermarket in #Tottenham in flames. (Riots spreading.) http://t.co/WOloxOt

PaulLewis : Sun Aug 07 02:29
Anyone still on the scene at #tottenham riot? Home now - reading Twitter stream - and tempted to go back.

PaulLewis : Sun Aug 07 02:33
The BBC's @rickin_majithia deserves credit for being the last journo (I know of) still at #tottenhamriot

PaulLewis : Sun Aug 07 02:35
Scrap that. BBC pulled out @rickin_majithia and all other reporters. Too dangerous.

PaulLewis : Sun Aug 07 02:42
Reports from @thethirdest (via @journodave) that riot spreading to Wood Green. Think I'm heading back out. #tottenham

PaulLewis : Sun Aug 07 02:47
RT @rickin_majithia: Police dogs being brought in. Rioters also using dogs. #Tottenham officer says a number of colleagues hospitalised.

PaulLewis : Sun Aug 07 02:52
Okay... Heading back. Any advice on where to go? #tottenham

PaulLewis : Sun Aug 07 03:15
Where in Wood Green? #tottenhamriot

PaulLewis : Sun Aug 07 03:21
Burned out bins forming barricades across Bruce Street. People in street shouting 'murderers' #tottenhamriot

Text R Letters to a friend

This text consists of extracts from two letters written by Ignatius Sancho, a London shopkeeper of African origin, to his friend John Spink about the Gordon Riots of 1780, an outbreak of civil disorder that led to several deaths and injuries in London.

Letter (a)

To JS ESQ.

Charles Street, June 6, 1780.

DEAR AND MOST RESPECTED SIR,

In the midst of the most cruel and ridiculous confusion, I am now set down to give you a very imperfect sketch of the maddest people that the maddest times were ever plagued with.—The public prints have informed you (without doubt) of last Friday's transactions;—the insanity of Ld G G and the worse than Negro barbarity of the populace;—the burnings and devastations of each night you will also see in the prints.

There is at this present moment at least a hundred thousand poor, miserable, ragged rabble, from twelve to sixty years of age, with blue cockades in their hats—besides half as many women and children—all parading the streets—the bridge—the park—ready for any and every mischief.—Gracious God! What's the matter now? I was obliged to leave off—the shouts of the mob—the horrid clashing of swords—and the clutter of a multitude in swiftest motion—drew me to the door—when every one in the street was employed in shutting up shop.—It is now just five o'clock—the ballad—singers are exhausting their musical talents—with the downfall of Popery, Sh, and Nh.—Lord Sh narrowly escaped with life about an hour since;—the mob seized his chariot going to the house, broke his glasses, and, in struggling to get his lordship out, they somehow have cut his face;—the guards flew to his assistance—the light-horse scowered the road, got his chariot, escorted him from the coffee-house, where he had fled for protection, to his carriage, and guarded him bleeding very fast home. This—this—is liberty! genuine British liberty!—This instant about two thousand liberty boys are swearing and swaggering by with large sticks—thus armed in hopes of meeting with the Irish chairmen and labourers—all the guards are out—and all the horse;—the poor fellows are just worn out for want of rest—having been on duty ever since Friday.—Thank heaven, it rains; may it increase, so as to send these deluded wretches safe to their homes, their families, and wives! About two this afternoon, a large party took it into their heads to visit the King and Queen, and entered the Park for that purpose—but found the guard too numerous to be forced, and after some useless attempts gave it up.—It is reported, the house will either be prorogued, or parliament dissolved, this evening—as it is in vain to think of attending any business while this anarchy lasts.

I am, dear Sir,
Yours ever by inclination,
IGN. SANCHO

Letter (b)

To JS ESQ.

Charles Street, June 9, 1780

MY DEAR SIR,

Government is sunk in lethargic stupor—anarchy reigns—when I look back to the glorious time of a George II. and a Pitt's administration—my heart sinks at the bitter contrast. We may now say of England, as was heretofore said of Great Babylon—"the beauty of the excellency of the Chaldees—is no more;"—the Fleet Prison, the Marshalsea, King's-Bench, both Compters, Clerkenwell, and Tothill Fields, with Newgate, are all slung open;—Newgate partly burned, and 300 felons from thence only let loose upon the world.—Lord M's house in town suffered martyrdom; and his sweet box at Caen Wood escaped almost miraculously, for the mob had just arrived, and were beginning with it—when a strong detachment from the guards and light-horse came most critically to its rescue—the library and, what is of more consequence, papers and deeds of vast value, were all cruelly consumed in the flames.—Ld. N's house was attacked; but they had previous notice, and were ready for them. The Bank, the Treasury, and thirty of the chief noblemen's houses, are doomed to suffer by the insurgents.—There were six of the rioters killed at Ld M's; and, what is remarkable, a daring chap escaped from Newgate, condemned to die this day, was the most active in mischief at Ld. M's, and was the first person shot by the soldier; so he found death a few hours sooner than if he had not been released.

I. SANCHO

The remainder in our next.

Half past nine o'clock.

King's-Bench prison is now in flames, and the prisoners at large; two fires in Holborn now burning.

Reproduced with thanks to Brycchan Carey

Exam-style question

You are allowed 15 minutes for planning and 1 hour for writing your answer to this question.

Referring to both texts in detail, and to relevant ideas from language study, analyse the ways language has changed over time.

48 marks

Plan your answer in the space below. Write your essay on separate sheets of paper and keep it with your workbook for reference.

Philip Allan, an imprint of Hodder Education, an Hachette UK company, Market Place, Deddington, Oxfordshire, OX15 0SE

Orders

Bookpoint Ltd, 130 Milton Park, Abingdon, Oxfordshire OX14 4SB

tel: 01235 827827 fax: 01235 400401

e-mail: education@bookpoint.co.uk

Lines are open 9.00 a.m.–5.00 p.m., Monday to Saturday, with a 24-hour message answering service. You can also order through the Philip Allan website: **www.philipallan.co.uk**

© Dan Clayton 2012

ISBN 978-1-4441-6456-5

First printed 2012

Impression number   5   4   3   2

Year   2017 2016 2015 2014 2013

Printed in Dubai

Hachette UK's policy is to use papers that are natural, renewable and recyclable products and made from wood grown in sustainable forests. The logging and manufacturing processes are expected to conform to the environmental regulations of the country of origin.

P02161

www.philipallan.co.uk

ISBN 978-1-4441-6456-5